ENERGY IN MOTION

AWAKEN

A

DREAM

dreamAwake
invites you
to create a name
for your friend

 _____ the turtle.

Similar to waves,
energy is constantly in motion.
When the mind holds onto energy,
emotions are created.
Emotions are an opportunity for transformation.
Let emotions be and let emotions go.
Allowing energy to flow,
creates space to grow!

Surf the waves of emotions
with your friend,
_____the turtle.
On this turtle speed journey
notice how energy comes and goes.
Celebrate feelings and emotions
using them as opportunities for transformation,
welcoming all the
AWESOME energy in the land!

Life tip from _____the turtle:
Gift yourself with loving kindness,
you deserve it!

One day far below the sand's surface
_____the turtle
was feeling
lonely and abandoned
inside its unhatched shell.
So _____the turtle
decided
the time is NOW
to break free from loneliness,
connect with the world outside,
smile with flowers,
dance with friends,
and surf the waves of life.

New to land and water
_____the turtle
was feeling gross and disgusted
in the salty sea.
So _____the turtle
decided
the time is NOW
to be grateful and enjoy the salt life,
accepting a salty, surfing invitation.
Salt water is great for skin, pain,
and cell hydration.

Standing at the ocean's edge,
noticing the water's rise and fall,
_____the turtle
was feeling worried and anxious
about the waves of life.
_____the turtle
decided
the time is NOW
to face worry and anxiety
discovering the buried treasure
of peace and contentment.
With peace and serenity,
_____the turtle
grabbed the surf board and
bravely learned
to ride the waves of life.

One sunny day
_____the turtle
felt a strong dislike
toward the sun for being so bright!
With not a cloud in the sky,
_____the turtle
decided
the time is NOW
to let go of dislike and create more love.
So _____the turtle
put on its groovy, shell hat
and sunshine love began to grow,
celebrating the gift of Vitamin D.
_____the turtle
rode the waves of life
with sunny style.

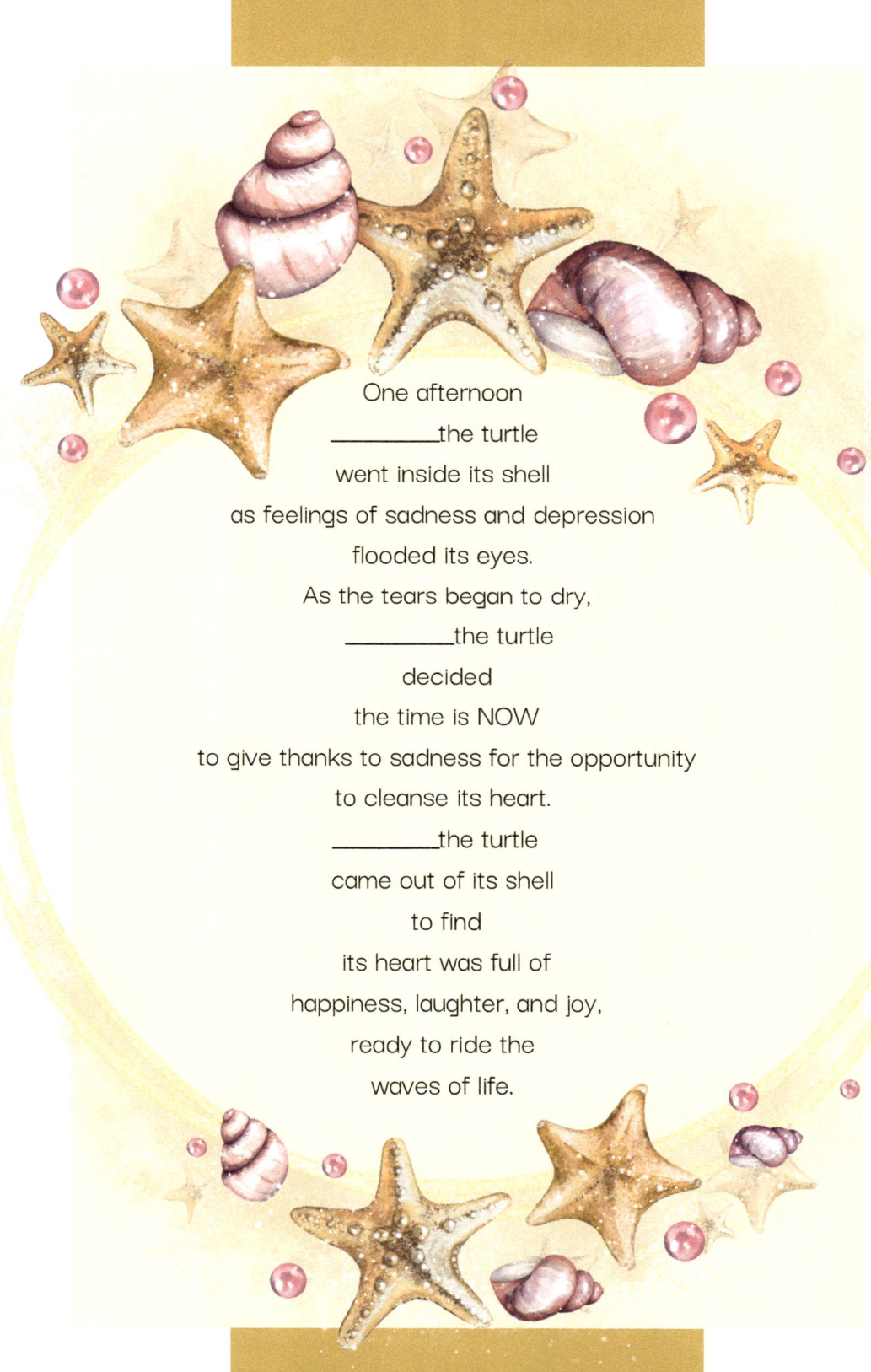

One afternoon
_____the turtle
went inside its shell
as feelings of sadness and depression
flooded its eyes.
As the tears began to dry,
_____the turtle
decided
the time is NOW
to give thanks to sadness for the opportunity
to cleanse its heart.
_____the turtle
came out of its shell
to find
its heart was full of
happiness, laughter, and joy,
ready to ride the
waves of life.

Standing on the beach
_____the turtle
was feeling hopeless and like a failure.
After 1, 2, and 3 tries
_____the turtle
still couldn't swim.
Gazing at the ocean,
_____the turtle
decided
the time is NOW
to feel hopeful and believe!
After the fourth, fifth, and sixth try,
_____the turtle
swam wild and free like a champion
with clown fish, dolphins, and manatees!

Life tip from _____the turtle:
Believe in your miraculous self
and you will make it!

One rainy day,
_____ the turtle
couldn't surf in the rain
and was feeling angry and mad.
_____ the turtle
decided
the time is NOW
to turn its frown upside down,
to dance in the rain
with compassion.
_____ the turtle
understood rain is a hydrating gift
for plants, flowers, and trees,
growing tall
with love for all.

After a long nap,
_____ the turtle
was feeling guilty and ashamed
for taking up space while resting on a rock.
Feeling those feelings,
_____the turtle
decided
the time is NOW
to let go of guilt,
practice forgiveness,
and grow forward.
_____ the turtle
thanked the rock for being
a stellar stage to
Rock 'n' Roll.

Sitting, watching for the waves of life to surf,
_____the turtle
felt frustrated and bored
at life's waiting game.
_____the turtle
decided
the time is NOW
to embrace the opportunity,
enjoy the calm waters,
and be patient.
To _____the turtle's
surprise
amazing waves began to arrive.

After riding the gnarly waves of life,
_____ the turtle
felt afraid and scared of falling
and began to question surfing.
Courageously,
_____ the turtle
decided
the time is NOW
to face fears and transform them,
accepting the chance of falling
as an opportunity
to swim with underwater friends.

When _____ the turtle
practices mindfulness,
it learns to listen and welcome any feeling.
_____ the turtle
decides
the time is NOW
to transform emotions
into energy in motion.
Letting emotions flow
to surf the waves of life!

Life tips from _____ the turtle:
Welcome emotions that arrive.
Decide the time is NOW!
Accept each emotion as an opportunity to grow.
Transform every emotion into something AMAZING!

EMOTIONAL TRANSFORMATION

loneliness and abandoned **AWAKENS** Connection and Unity

gross and disgusted **AWAKENS** Grateful and Thankful

worried and anxious **AWAKENS** Peace and Contentment

dislike AWAKENS Love

sadness and depression **AWAKENS** Happiness, Laughter, and Joy

hopeless and failure AWAKENS Hopeful and Believe

anger and mad **AWAKENS** Compassion and Understanding

guilty and ashamed **AWAKENS** Forgiveness and Sympathy

frustrated and bored **AWAKENS** Patience and Surprise

fear and afraid **AWAKENS** Courage and Bravery

www.ingramcontent.com/pod-product-compliance
Lightning Source LLC
Chambersburg PA
CBHW042040050526
44107CB00107B/1041